A Victorian Visit 1

In the late 19th century, Brighton .. _ _ super-Mare'. Fast and luxurious rail services meant that wealthy businessmen could live by the sea and work in the Metropolis and Britain's expanding railway network enabled thousands of holiday makers from all parts of the Country to visit the resort and enjoy its unique attractions.

Detailed guide-books were available to help tourists make the most of their visit, with sections on its history, geology, weather, where to stay and places of interest …. in fact, just about everything they could want or need to know.

This booklet combines text relating to Brighton from 'Black's Guide to Sussex', published in 1896, with photographs taken from postcards and 'magic lantern' projection slides, owned by the Keasbury-Gordon Photograph Archive.

It is in three parts. The first comprises sixteen photographs taken between 1880 and 1920, the second, a history and general description of Sussex and the third, a detailed exploration of Brighton. The text for parts two and three is reproduced from the 1896 guide-book. The original book has considerable 'foxing' (brown, age-related stains), which appear on the pages of this booklet as dark marks and patches.

The photographs and text complement each other and enable us to travel back in time to visit Britain's 'Queen of Resorts'. I hope you enjoy the journey.

Andrew Gill

The Sea Serpent, Gloucester Road

The Royal Chain Pier

The Aquarium

The Beach

Black Lion Street

Central Railway Station

Royal Chain Pier

The Grand Hotel

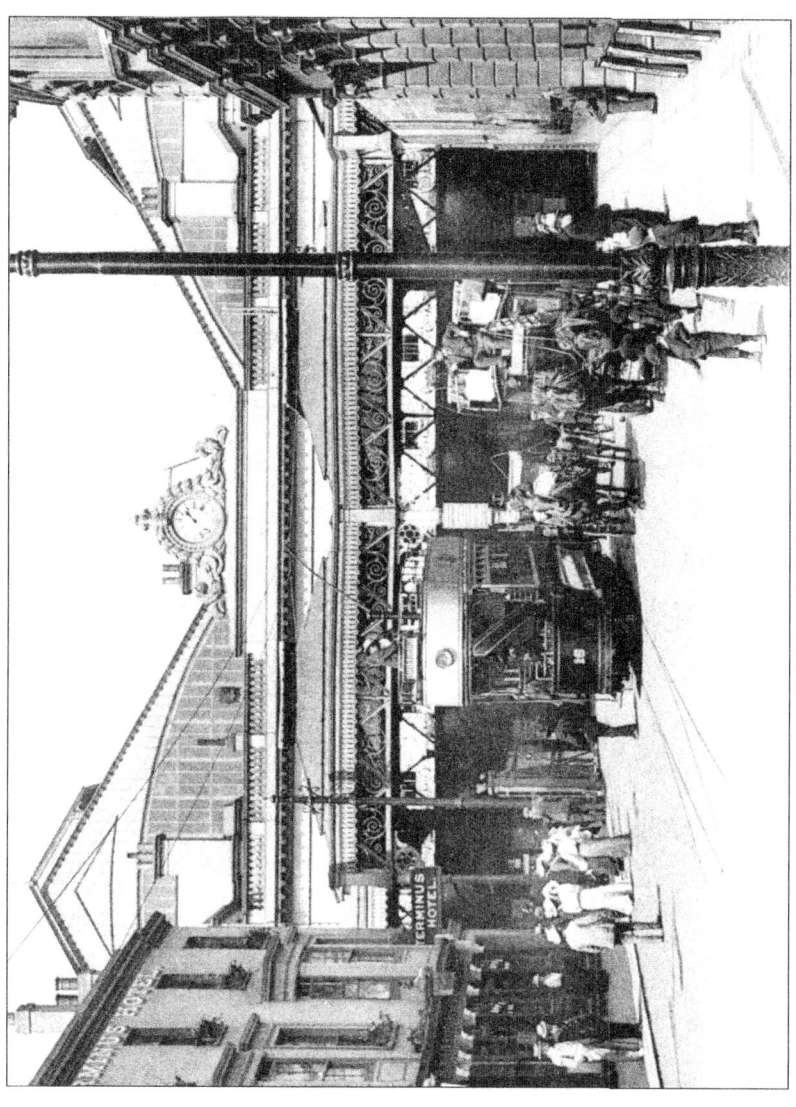

The Railway Station

Trip 'round the Bay

Brighton Corporation Trams

Veteran cars at the Hotel Metropole

The Beach

Volk's Electric Railway

The Brighton and Rottingdean Seashore
Electric Railway

'Jack and Jill' Windmills, Clayton near Brighton

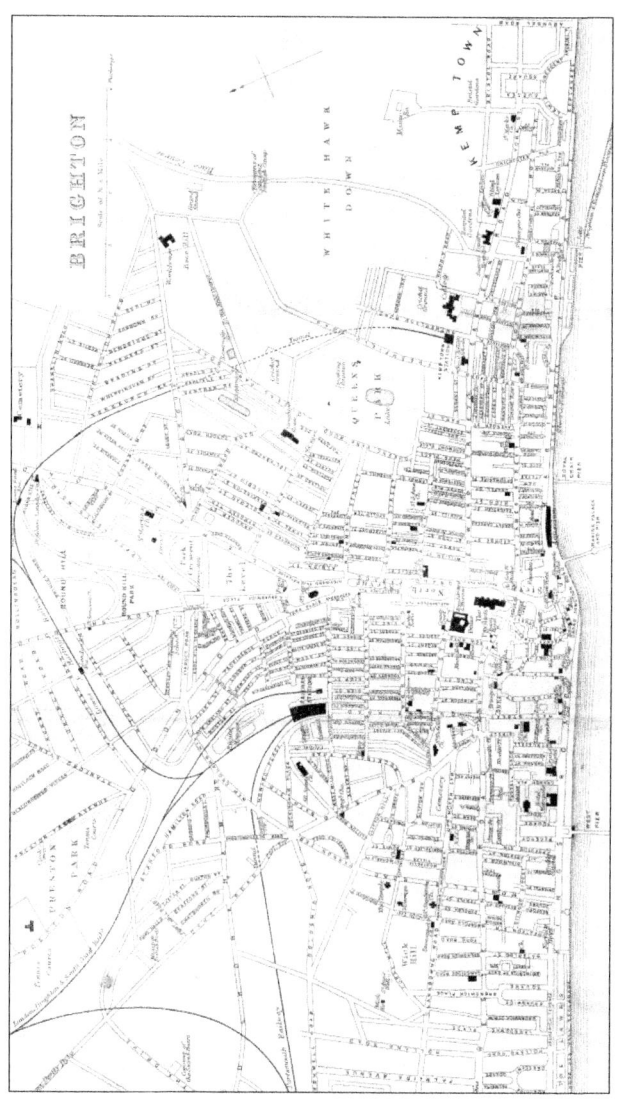

Brighton in 1896

INTRODUCTION

THE county of Sussex consists of an oblong territory, stretching along the southern coast of England, bounded on the west by Hampshire; on the north, north-east, and east by Surrey and Kent. The line of its coast, following the indentations, is nearly 90 miles long; the extreme length of the county in a straight line, from Ladyholt Park on the west, to the end of Kent Ditch on the east, is 76 miles; the extreme breadth, in a cross line from Tunbridge Wells on the north to Beachy Head on the south, 27 miles. It contains 933,269 acres, and is inhabited by a population which, according to the census of 1891, amounted to 550,446.

The whole district is divided into 6 rapes, 73 hundreds, and 312 civil parishes, containing 7 municipal boroughs, viz. Arundel, Chichester, Hastings, and Rye (by ancient title), Brighton (incorporated 1854), Lewes (1881), and Eastbourne (1883). Winchelsea, Seaford, Pevensey, and Midhurst were unreformed corporations existing under old charters; the first governed by a mayor and the latter three by bailiffs, but their privileges have been abolished. By the Redistribution of Seats Bill (1885) the parliamentary representation of Sussex is divided among 9 members—6 from rural constituencies, 2 from the

INTRODUCTION

borough of Brighton, and 1 from that of Hastings. But before the Reform Bill of 1832, Sussex returned no less than 28 members, and contained several "rotten" boroughs.

The *rape* is a division peculiar to Sussex, and not found in any other English county. The origin of the term has caused much discussion, but it is probably derived from the Icelandic *hreppr*, signifying land divided by a rope. There is no evidence of its existence before the Conquest, and it was doubtless introduced by the Normans, as it is first mentioned in the *Domesday Survey*. The rapes are Hastings, Pevensey, and Lewes in East Sussex, and Bramber, Arundel, and Chichester in West Sussex, their boundaries extending from the northern limit of the county to the coast. Each formerly enclosed one of the six military high roads to Normandy, and contained a castle, situate on a river or close to the sea.

Ecclesiastically the county is coextensive with the diocese of Chichester, subdivided into the archdeaconries and 11 rural deaneries of Lewes and Chichester. There are two County Councils, for East and West Sussex.

Physical Aspects.—The county is made up of two natural divisions very differently characterised, the coast and the Wealden district, lying south and north respectively. The coast is shut in by the South Downs, keeping, for the most part, parallel with the sea, a few miles behind it, till they end at the bold promontory of Beachy Head. This stretch of heights, between 40 and 50 miles long, broken here and there into blocks by the river valleys, has an average height of 500 feet, but at some points they swell up to over 800 feet. Ditchling Beacon (813 feet) is commonly spoken of as the highest point; but the latest *Ordnance Survey* gives a few feet more to Linch Ball, near the Hampshire border.

INTRODUCTION

The beauty of these "soft bosomy eminences" is quite their own. They have been compared to green waves of land copying its neighbour, the sea; and Mr. Harrison Ainsworth is not the only writer who has risen into enthusiasm over them. "No breeze so fresh and invigorating as that of these Sussex Downs; no turf so springy to the foot as their soft greensward! A flock of larks flies past us, and a cloud of mingled rooks and starlings wheels overhead. Mark you little T-shaped cuttings on the slope below us—those are the snares set by the shepherds for the delicious wheat-ear, our English ortolan. The fairies still haunt this spot, and hold their midnight revels upon it, as yon dark green rings testify. The common folk hereabouts term the good people 'Pharisees,' and style these emerald circles 'hay tracks.' Why, we care not to inquire. Enough for us, the fairies are not altogether gone. A smooth soft carpet is here spread out for Oberon and Titania, and their attendant elves, to dance upon by moonlight; and there is no lack of mushrooms to form tables for 'Puck's banquets.'"

Even Harrison Ainsworth admits—though Gilbert White does not—that the South Downs want boldness and grandeur. To some their gentle softness has an effect of monotony; and, perhaps, one must grow familiar with them fully to enter into their peculiar charms, not as generally relished as the flavour of their mutton. One hill is often so like another that the stranger may easily go astray for want of landmarks to guide him to the scattered villages lying hidden in cup-like hollows. Thick weather here might make a real danger for bewildered wanderers, who in such a case are advised to orient themselves by noting the inclination of any timber exposed to the pre-

INTRODUCTION

valent south-west winds, and how its sheltered side is more likely to be stained by lichen.

As a rule, the Downs themselves have a bolder face to the north, while they slope more gently on the sea-side, where the flat strip at their foot has suffered much from incursions of the waves. The site of the ancient cathedral of Selsey is now a mile out at sea. Between 1292 and 1340 A.D. upwards of 5500 acres were submerged. In the early part of the 14th century Pagham Harbour was formed by a sudden irruption of the sea, devastating 2700 acres, which recently have been reclaimed and again brought under cultivation. There is reason for believing that the whole coast-line of the county has been slightly raised in the last 800 years (possibly by earthquake shock), as the large estuaries at the river mouths no longer exist, and the archipelago of knolls round Pevensey (*eye* signifies "island") have only a slight elevation above the neighbouring marsh land.

Upon the north edge of the county, facing the Downs, runs more irregularly a sandy and well-wooded range of heights, known as the Forest Ridge, which turns southward beyond Tunbridge Wells, reaching the coast at Fairlight, near Hastings. Almost all the extent of this ridge offers beautiful scenery of a more varied type. The broken plain between, often rising into picturesque heights, was once thickly covered by forests, as its name of *Weald* implies. Here, till the 17th century, were the great ironworks of England, now transferred to the neighbourhood of coal-fields. The once famed Wealden forests, however, are not yet exhausted; considerable patches of them still remain, often as ornaments of the lordly parks forming such a frequent feature in Sussex, which contains no less than four ducal seats,

INTRODUCTION

and many others about which art has vied with nature to please the eye. There are few parts of England that make up a richer picture than the Weald of Sussex, with its mingled display of hill and dale, rich meadows, and wild commons, weathered cottages and noble mansions, backed by fine foliage and bold eminences.

In one kind of scenery the county is deficient. The rivers are short, and for the most part rather prosaic in their quiet course, generally southward. The least unimportant are the two Rothers, the Arun, the Adur, the Ouse, the Cuckmere, and the upper waters of the Medway.

Geology.—A great portion of the county is occupied by the Chalk formation, of which the South Downs are almost entirely composed. Firestone is found in the west, and Steyning is built upon it. At the base of the Downs the Greensand crops up, but is of small extent. The Wealden formations occupy nearly all the inland district of the county, and in these occurs the ironstone from which iron was extracted. Sussex was at one time the centre of the English iron manufacture; before 1653 there were 42 iron forges or mills (reduced to 18 before 1667) and 27 furnaces (reduced to 11 before 1664), which employed 50,000 men and furnished the main supply of ordnance for the national defence. The last forge at Ashburnham was not extinguished until 1809. Between 1872 and 1876 boring was carried on at Netherfield, near Battle, with the object of discovering what beds were below the Wealden, and if possible of reaching the Palæozoic rocks, which at Kentish Town, Harwich, Ostend, and Calais had been found at a depth of about 1000 feet below the sea-level. Some slight hope was entertained of the occurrence of Coal Measures, as in the

INTRODUCTION

Boulonnais the Carboniferous Limestone, where last seen, dips south. The boring was continued to a depth of 1905 feet, the Oxford Clay being reached. The chief result was the discovery of the unusual thickness of the Kimmeridge Clay, which began at 275 feet from the surface and continued to a depth of about 1469 feet. The most practical result was the finding of thick beds of gypsum (at about 160 feet), which were before unknown in the Weald, and are now worked at Netherfield. From Beachy Head to Selsey Bill there lies, south of the Downs, a low and level tract belonging to the Tertiary period, of which there is no such record at any other place in England. The towns of Hove, Worthing, Littlehampton, Bognor, etc., are built on gravel, sand, and loam of the Post-Pliocene or Pleistocene series, which superficial beds overlie the Eocene series in patches and contain a large fossil fauna. Remains of the mammoth occur in the mud deposit (or *Lutraria* clay) of this district, and the Chichester Museum contains the greater portion of a fine skeleton of the *Elephas antiquus* obtained off Selsey Bill. Of the British Quaternary fossils 45 are peculiar to Selsey, and 20 others probably find here their earliest place in British geological history. The Bracklesham beds occur at the bay of that name, their main divisions extending from Wittering on the west to the Barn Rocks, east of Selsey Bill, a distance of 7 miles. They are full of fossil shells, particularly nummulitic.

Flora.—An analysis of the flora of the county was placed before the British Association in 1872 by Mr. W. B. Hemsley (*Report*, 1872, p. 128), who stated the total number of indigenous plants to be 1000, to which 59 introduced species must be added. The most interesting features of the flora are the number of species to the

INTRODUCTION

county area, the species peculiar to certain formations, viz. the Chalk (56), maritime species (76), and the rare species, especially of the Atlantic and Scottish types. Amongst the rarer marsh plants are *Isnardia palustris, Scirpus triqueter, S. carinatus, Pyrola media, Habeneria albida, Festuca sylvatica* of the "Scottish" type of Watson; this last is not found in adjoining counties. A prominent feature of the Wealden flora is the extent of heath land and the large size the heath attains.

History and Antiquities. — The earliest known settlers here were the Celtic tribes, whose memorials are found in the hill-forts of Mount Caburn, Hollingbury, White Hawk, Ditchling Beacon, Devil's Dyke, Chanctonbury Hill, Cissbury, etc., the latter being a great factory for flint implements. They gave the names to the rivers. Little is, however, known of them beyond the fact that they had a distinct coinage some two centuries before the Roman invasion,—a coarse imitation of the Greek *stater* of Philip II. of Macedon. These coins have been found in various parts of Sussex. At the time of Cæsar's landing (55 B.C.) the Belgic tribe of the Regni inhabited the county and had their capital at Regnum (Chichester). Sir G. B. Airy fixed on Pevensey as the place of Cæsar's landings in 55 and 54 B.C.; this is, however, much disputed, and opinion generally puts the landing near Deal. A few years after this Sussex appears to have formed part of the kingdom of Commius, a British chieftain, and upon his death seems to have been allotted to his son Tincommius. These two are the only British rulers of the county whose coins have been found.

Upon the conquest of Britain under Claudius, the Romans found a ready tool in a king named Cogidubnus, mentioned by Tacitus, who was created imperial legate,

INTRODUCTION

and may probably be identified with the king of that name mentioned in the celebrated inscription on the temple of Neptune and Minerva found at Chichester. Sussex was conquered prior to the reign of Vespasian, and Major-General Pitt-Rivers suggests that the hill-fort of Mount Caburn may have been one of the twenty *oppida* Suetonius states to have been reduced by that emperor. Roman settlements became numerous in the county, and villas sprang up, the remains of which are still occasionally found, the chief being that at Bignor, near Stane Street, the Roman road connecting Chichester with London, still partly traceable. A fortress was erected at Anderida (Pevensey), and there was another town named Mutuantonis, which is thought to be Lewes; but it may have been situated farther west than Lewes, perhaps at Littlehampton.

Sussex was the first county invaded by the Saxons, who in 477 landed under Ælle at Keynor, near Chichester. After fourteen years of struggle they reached the point where the South Downs abut on the sea at Beachy Head, and in 491, as the *Saxon Chronicle* grimly records, "Ælle and Cissa beset Andredes-ceaster (Anderida), and slew all that were therein, nor was there a Briton left there any more." This resulted in the formation of a distinct kingdom of South Saxons, whence its name of *Sussex*. The subjugation of the county was very complete, for it is still one of the most thoroughly Saxon counties in England, and its inhabitants, speech, place-names, customs, etc., are almost entirely Saxon.

The next important event in the history of the county was the landing of William of Normandy (28th September 1066), followed by the battle of Senlac or Hastings (14th October 1066). The Conqueror erected on the

INTRODUCTION

battlefield an abbey dedicated to St. Martin, but this was not completed until after his death. Then came the great battle of Lewes between Henry III. and the barons under Simon de Montfort in 1264, which " wiped out the stain—if stain it were—of Senlac." Other important events have been the rebellion of Jack Cade in 1450, which received substantial support in East Sussex, and the naval engagement fought off Beachy Head in 1690, in which the English and Dutch fleets combined were defeated by the French. Charles II. in his flight after the battle of Worcester escaped in 1651 from Shoreham in a fishing-boat.

The foremost place amongst the illustrious natives of Sussex must be assigned to Shelley the poet. As statesmen we have John Selden and Richard Cobden, and as eminent ecclesiastics Archbishops Frewen and William Juxon, also Archdeacon Hare. Its poets include Thomas Otway, Thomas Sackville (afterwards Earl of Dorset), and John Fletcher. Among its antiquaries we find Sir William Burrell, John Elliot, Rev. Thomas W. Horsfield, Mark Antony Lower, Dr. Mantell (geologist), and Dr. Richard Russell (founder of modern Brighton).

Dialect.—A large number of Saxon words are still retained and pronounced in the old style; thus *gate* becomes *ge-at*. The letter *a* is very broad in all words, as if followed by *u*, and in fact converts words of one syllable into words of two, as *faüs* (face), *taüst* (taste), etc. Again, *a* before double *d* becomes *ar*, as *arder* and *larder* for *adder* and *ladder;* oi is like a long *i*, as *spile* (spoil), *intment* (ointment); an *e* is substituted for *a* in such words as *rag*, *flag*, etc. The French refugees in the 16th and 17th centuries introduced many words which are still in common use: a Sussex woman

INTRODUCTION

when unprepared to receive visitors says she is in *dishabille* (déshabillé, undress); if her child is unwell it looks *pekid* (piqué), if fretful is a little *peter-grievous* (petit-grief); she cooks with a *broach* (broche, a spit), and talks of *coasts* (coste, Old French) or ribs of meat, etc. There is an excellent *Dictionary of the Sussex Dialect*, by the Rev. W. D. Parish. As the names occur, we have pointed out local peculiarities of pronunciation that puzzle a stranger.

Climate.—The two districts of Sussex show a considerable contrast of climate—the Weald wetter and more in extremes, while the coast has greater equability and dryness, the annual rainfall here being 10 inches less than north of the Downs. Sussex, above all other parts of the English coast, seems to unite the two qualities of brightness and bracingness; certainly there is none within easy reach of London that enjoys such an amount of winter sunshine along with a tonic air where the cold is usually tempered, yet not to the relaxing mildness of our south-western resorts, with which Hastings alone may vie in this respect by its sheltered situation. All along the Sussex coast, then, there have sprung up a row of the most flourishing watering-places in the kingdom, Brighton the chief of them; and this, though the shore is far from beautiful or grand, unless at a few points, like Fairlight and Beachy Head.

To these crowded resorts and their vicinity we have given most space, on our principle of the greatest good of the greatest number. But we have not failed to guide our readers about the more numerous if less frequented centres of the northern district; and we believe that no place of note has been left unmentioned, at least in

INTRODUCTION

outline. Some lovely parts of the county are so little visited that, in the interest of the majority, we are conscious of not having done them justice. Still, whoever follows up all our more or less detailed indications, might say, as truly as Tennyson's *Harold*, "I know all Sussex!"

Railways.—The traversing of this county, which active pedestrians and cyclists can cross at a stretch, is facilitated by numerous railway lines, not to speak of the driving trips and excursion steamers plying in summer from places like Brighton and Hastings. In each section we have been careful to show the communications and opportunities for getting about. On its west and east sides, respectively, Sussex is touched by branches of the London and South-Western and of the South-Eastern Railway systems. But it mainly depends on the London, Brighton, and South Coast Railway, which, throughout nearly the whole county, has a monopoly of the traffic on its several lines and branches. There is no lack of trains on these, especially in the summer season; and by certain of them advantage can be taken of cheap fares, for which the Company's programmes may be studied. On the other hand, complaints are often made of unpunctuality, and sometimes of incivility on the part of porters, perhaps spoiled by the abundant "tips" of the great watering-places.

Hostelries here are of all sorts, from the palatial hotels of Brighton and Eastbourne to the unpretentious village inns, which often offer quite as much real comfort to travellers of simple tastes.

THE BRIGHTON ROAD

Both by road and rail there is more than one way to Brighton. The main line, on which the express trains run, traverses Surrey by Croydon and Red Hill, entering Sussex a little north of *Three Bridges Junction,* where branches go off on the left for *East Grinstead* and *Tunbridge Wells,* on the right for *Horsham,* through all of which places an alternative route might be taken by leisurely travellers. These branches will be followed in our *Wealden Forests* section.

From *Three Bridges* the main line runs almost straight across the county, so as to show its varied characteristics successively displayed in half an hour. On the north side we are carried through *Tilgate Forest,* a stretch of undulating timber, heath, and sand, largely enclosed as parks, and where red modern villas form a frequent contrast to the weather-worn cottages of old Sussex. A tunnel takes us into more open scenery beyond **Balcombe** (*Bawkum* in rural mouths), a quiet village with an Early English church, lying at the foot of the Wealden Hills. The country now, though more varied, is still richly wooded and beautifully broken.

To the left of the line will catch the eye *Ardingly*

College, the third of Canon Woodward's schools (see *Lancing*), where boys are educated for £18 a year, more after the manner of Winchester than of Dotheboys Halls. *Ardingly* is the single way-station of a short branch which presently unites *Hayward's Heath* with *Horsted Keynes* on the line between *East Grinstead* and *Lewes*. Note here, once for all, that the termination *ly* in Sussex must be strongly accented *lie* by those who would not betray themselves as strangers.

The bottom of the Sussex *Ouse* is now crossed by a viaduct, and soon we reach **Hayward's Heath** (*Station Hotel*; small temperance inn on the other side of the line; and *Oakwood* Select Boarding House), which is the centre of the county, and for more than one reason deserves to be stopped at. Standing high on sandy soil, with the advantage of being a railway junction for Lewes and East Grinstead, it has grown so much of late years as to weigh down its neighbour, *Cuckfield*, joined with it to make up a population of about 5000. The building of many scattered villas and bits of streets has much cut up the heath, part of which will be found, to the east of the station, laid out as a pleasure-ground with paths and seats. Above this, still to the left of the line, the restored church of *St. Wilfrid* stands on an eminence of 300 feet, well called the "Copestone of Sussex," to which converge all the lines of the Ordnance Survey. From the churchyard there is a good view southwards.

In this direction the place straggles on for a mile or more past *Hazelgrove Park* to the *County Lunatic Asylum*, a conspicuous building in large grounds, by which another mile or so brings us to the well-timbered village of **Wivelsfield**, with its Early English church, whence we could turn off to the next station, *Burgess Hill*, or walk on in about a dozen miles to Brighton.

On the same side of the line, about 2 miles north-east, is the picturesquely embowered little town of **Lindfield** (*Tiger* and *Red Lion Inns*), among many beautiful nooks of scenery, and fine old mansions, such as *Paxhill*. The upper waters of the *Ouse* hereabouts are known to anglers,

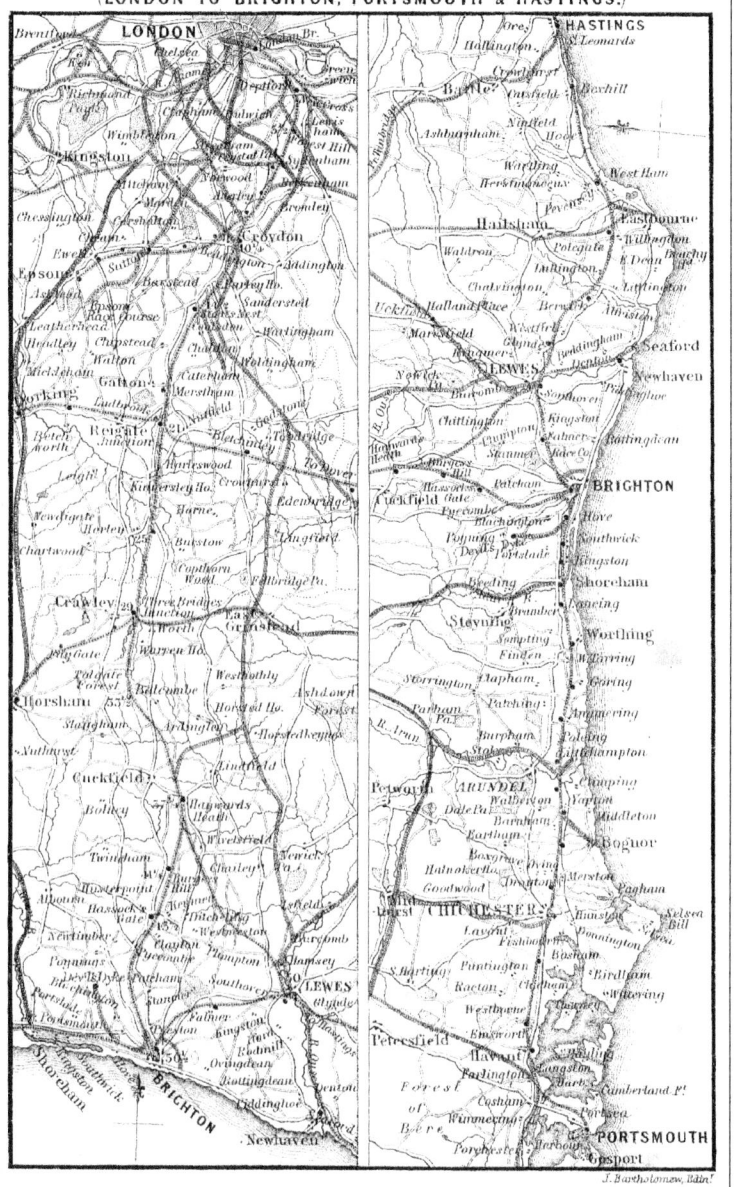

with whom the *Sloop Inn* at **Freshfield**, about 4 miles from Hayward's Heath, is a favourite resort.

Cuckfield (Hotels : *Talbot* (C.), *King's Arms*) lies 2 miles to the west of *Hayward's Heath*. An omnibus runs several times a day between the two places ; and the shady road has a paved side walk and gas-lamps all the way. Turn up the hill from the *Station Hotel*, bearing round on the right of the *Green* by the *Sergison Arms*. Coming thus into the middle of the pleasant little town (pron. *Cookfield*), turn down to the left for the hotels and the restored Early English church, with ivied tower and spire, containing interesting memorials and monuments by Flaxman and Westmacott. From the enlarged churchyard there is a good view across to the South Downs.

Cuckfield Place and park, with its fine avenue, extend just beyond the church, on the other side of the road. This Elizabethan mansion is the *Rookwood Hall* of Harrison Ainsworth's romance, the "Doomtree," which figures there, being still preserved in the avenue. The park is open to the public only on Sundays and holidays ; but a right-of-way runs across the top of it ; and an hour's walk might be suggested that would give a good glimpse of the country. This path leads off to the right through a wicket gate at the end of the town, to wind pleasantly westward over the broken and timbered ground, till after a long mile it brings one to a leafy lane that, taken to the right, would carry one by a considerable circuit by *Whiteman's Green* into the upper part of Cuckfield ; or to the left, would lead in a mile to *Ansty's Cross* (cross roads), where a sharp turn to the left would complete the triangle back into Cuckfield. Were one to follow the road south from Ansty's Cross, it would soon be found dividing, the right branch for *Hurstpierpoint*, on which in a mile or so is passed *Leigh Pond*, one of the largest sheets of water in the county ; the left branch for *St. John's Common* and *Burgess Hill*. Through Cuckfield and Hurstpierpoint runs one of the alternative roads from London to Brighton.

Hayward's Heath has become a place of family residence

even for Londoners. The next places on this railway might be called the Croydon and Norwood of Brighton. First comes *Keymer Junction*, where the line goes off for Lewes, Eastbourne, and Hastings, but the local trains start at *Hayward's Heath*. Why *Keymer?* might well be asked, as the village of this name lies farther south than the next station, **Burgess Hill** (*Railway* and *Burgess Hill Inns* beside the station). Brick-making is carried on here, and the bricks are largely made into snug homes for Brighton business men and others, spreading roomily over St. John's Common, but not altogether destroying the rural charms of this neighbourhood.

The Downs now come full into view, rising steeply across our way. A mile from the foot of them is **Hassocks** (Hotels: *Hassocks Gate* at the station, *Downs* and *Clayton Park* (C.) in the neighbourhood, the former describing itself as a "bijou hotel," the latter more of a popular resort), which, with the adjacent villages on either side, is almost a suburb of Brighton. Omnibuses run several times a day, eastward to *Keymer* and *Ditchling*, which we shall visit from Brighton ; and westward to **Hurstpierpoint** (*New Inn* (C.), *Sussex Arms*), 2 miles off, a pretty village, or rather town, of nearly 3000 people. There is a fine view from the rebuilt church, which, besides some time-worn memorials, contains a tablet to *Bishop Hannington*, born here and martyred at Uganda 1885. The *Chinese Gardens* are a popular resort for picnics and school treats. *Danny Park*, with its venerable oaks, lies under the Downs to the south-east ; and behind the Elizabethan brick mansion rise *Wolstanbury Hill*, crowned with a circular Celtic encampment. To the north-east is *St. John's College*, the second of the Woodward schools, a Gothic building, whose unfinished chapel contains a fine reredos and some good glass. Both school and parish are, in colloquial speech, *Hurst*, i.e. wood, a name that well bespeaks the charm of the country.

Beyond *Hassocks* the railway pierces the Downs by *Clayton Tunnel*, at the further end of which another belt

BRIGHTON

of wood soon gives place to bare swells topped by the outskirts of Brighton, reached at the suburban station of *Preston Park.*

The coaches (*fares:* inside, 10s. ; outside, 15s. ; box seat, 20s.) which, from May to October, run three times a week in each direction between the *Hotel Victoria,* Northumberland Avenue, London, and the *Old Ship,* Brighton, take a line a few miles to the west of the railway, for the most part passing much the same scenery. Through Surrey, indeed, the route is almost identical ; but beyond Horley, where a halt is made for lunch, the road bears off to the right, entering Sussex at *County Oak,* a little beyond which it traverses *Crawley,* of which we shall speak elsewhere, to mount a long ascent. Horses are changed at the oddly named *Pease Pottage,* then come *Handcross* (where the road through *Cuckfield* goes off), *Bolney,* and *Albourne Green,* where, again, a mile or so's divagation to the left would bring us to *Hurstpierpoint.* Now we are full in face of the South Downs, which the coach passes by *Pyecombe,* avoiding the steep ascent of *Clayton Hill,* and through *Patcham* descends into Brighton by the gardens of the *Steyne,* the journey, begun at noon, taking just six hours.

Cyclists have a choice of roads to Brighton, for which their own guides are more explicit than we can afford to be.

BRIGHTON

Railway: Brighton is rather over 50 miles from London by the London, Brighton, and South Coast Railway, which does so much of its traffic with this terminus that it goes by the popular name of the Brighton Line: Metropolitan Stations, *Victoria* and *London Bridge.* Brighton has three stations: the *Central,* behind the middle of the town ; *Hove,* for the west part, to which some trains run direct ; and *Kemp Town,* for the east end, reached by a branch from the Central terminus ; besides the stopping stations of *Preston Park* and *Lewes Road* in the north suburbs. The journey is, or ought to be, done by express trains in less than an hour and a half. By certain trains in the day there are cheap return fares ; and such tickets are also given at Brighton for neighbouring places of interest. Ordinary fares from London: 1st class, 10s. ; 2nd class, 6s. 6d. ; 3rd class, 4s. 2½d.

Omnibuses run from the Central Station to various parts of the town.

BRIGHTON

Carriages: Fares range from 1s. a mile, or 3s. an hour for a "first-class carriage," *i.e.* an ordinary cab, to 6d. a mile for a "fourth-class carriage"—a goat chaise for children. Double fares at night.

Hotels: Along the sea front (arranged from west to east), mostly first class and expensive—*Norfolk, Bedford, Metropole, Grand, Hamblin's, Old Ship, Harrison's, Star and Garter, Markwell's, Queen's, Clarendon, Lion Mansion, York, Albion, Pier, Albemarle* (C.), *Haxell's, Crescent, Bristol.—Sillwood Hall,* and *New Steine* look to the sea, but stand a little way back.

At Hove, *Prince's, Sussex*.

In the town: *New Ship, Gloucester* (C.), *Clarence, Castle, White Lion, Garden* (Temperance), etc.

There are several temperance and other cheap "hotels" in the road leading from the Railway Station. It may be mentioned that the good old houses, such as the *Bedford, Albion, Old Ship*, hold their own here, though the gigantic caravansaries, more recently established by Limited Companies, recommend themselves to a certain class of visitors.

It is impossible to enumerate all the Private Hotels and Boarding Houses which abound here, chiefly on the sea front and about the West Pier. Many of them hardly differ from ordinary hotels, several holding a licence. We fear to do an injustice in selecting some score names of all classes, to which application might be made for terms, ranging from 30s. to 80s. per week. The *Dudley, Como House, Milton Hall, Marlborough, Haslemere, Melrose Hall, Cavendish Mansion, Devonshire House, Connaught House, The Carlton, St. Edmunds, Portland House, Brighton House, Fitzroy House, Eastcote House, Stanstead House, Bank House, Kingsville, Argyle Mansion, Warwick Mansion, Detraz's Private Hotel, Madeira House, Chichester Mansion, Blenheim House, Lancaster House, Sussex House, Saville House,* etc. etc. These, again, are somewhat roughly placed according to position, beginning at the west end, the last three or four standing back from the sea about the Pavilion.

Lodgings: To be obtained in all parts, those at the sea front naturally the most expensive, those in the upper parts of the town cheaper.

The **General Post Office** in *Ship Street*, running inland from the front, about half-way between the two piers.

London-super-Mare is the nickname of this town, the metropolis of English sea-side resorts, looked up to by every ambitious provincial watering-place that advertises itself as a local Brighton. It is connected with London by a service of frequent, fast, and luxurious trains. The passengers travelling by the morning Pullman express are said to be the most moneyed crew committed to the care of any railway company, so that the idea of accident to such a train appeals powerfully to even a Stock Exchange imagination. Brighton is the home, indeed, of many busy city men, as well as the sojourn of idlers, and a familiar visiting-place to many others, who run down here for at least a "week end" to breathe a purer air than can be found in Oxford Street or Cheapside, not to speak of the still larger class of London excursionists, with whom this is the favourite goal for a day's outing.

Brighton's enemies have some justice in disparaging it as a mere suburb of the capital, loved by Cockneys who wish as little as possible to change their habits and society. It is certainly overgrown far beyond the homely retirement which makes some people's *beau ideal* of a sea-side holiday. Another charge brought against it is the scarcity of trees to relieve the monotony of stucco and plate glass. The country about, but for two or three choice nooks, is bare and dull. But when all drawbacks are stated, there remains the fact of Brighton's popularity with almost every class. Perhaps the main attraction, beyond the hotels, the shops, the general stir of pleasure and expense, is the large share of sunshine and bracing air at once that comes to this corner of the coast.

Brighton ranks as one of the oldest of our sea-side resorts, which is not saying much. Till about the middle of last century, under its uncontracted name of *Brighthelmston*, of which eighty-four different spellings have been collected, it was a more or less obscure fishing-town, with records of suffering, like its neighbours, from inroads of the sea and attacks of the French. The chief note in its history is Charles II. having hence made his escape to France after the battle of Worcester. The help Brighton gave thus to one prince was effectually repaid by another. George IV. as Prince of Wales took a fancy to the place; and his patronage went far towards its prosperity, if not its morality. The Duke of Cumberland, hero of Culloden, had been a still earlier visitor. But the medical profession were the real founders of Brighton's rise and progress. In 1750 Dr. Russell, from Lewes, settled here to be the first of the eminent practitioners who have brought patients from London to the Steyne. Literary men have also shown a weakness for Brighton. Dr. Johnson, indeed, grumbled, *more suo*, declaring the country "so desolate, that if one had a mind to hang oneself for desperation at being obliged to live there, it would be difficult to find a tree on which to fasten a rope." Charles Lamb, also, did not find this place enough like London. But other famous writers have been more friendly, Thackeray in particular. "It is the fashion," says he, "to run down George IV., but what myriads of Londoners ought to thank him for inventing Brighton ! One of the best physicians our city has ever known, is kind, cheerful, merry Dr. Brighton. Hail, thou purveyor of shrimps, and honest prescriber of South Down mutton ; no fly so pleasant as Brighton flies ; nor any cliffs so pleasant to ride on ; no shops so beautiful to look at as the Brighton gimcrack shops, and the fruit shops, and the market!" Dickens also celebrates Brighton, though hardly with the same enthusiasm ; he seems to find fault with all the fine folk for not listening to what the wild waves are saying. Among our contemporary novelists, Mr. William Black has shown his admiration by making his home here, along with more than one celebrity of the journalistic world. Miss Florence Marryat and "Edna Lyall," whatever they may think of it, were at all events born at Brighton.

The railway, perhaps, had the largest hand in making Brighton's fortune. It is now a place of over 140,000 inhabitants, counting in Hove, its western annexe. The average number of visitors has been stated at 30,000 ; but it seems impossible to estimate how many strangers come to Brighton in the course of the year, during which myriads of excursionists are so often turned out to lose themselves in its lively thoroughfares. Their great time is the early months of summer, when Brighton is rather deserted by more fastidious visitors. But it is never empty of strangers, enjoying a succession of seasons, the most fashionable that of the late autumn and up to Christmas. The worst time here is that of the cold spring months, when east winds would be found trying in the more unsheltered parts. From another point of view, the "Sussex fortnight" at the end of July is a time to be avoided by those who do not admire the company brought from far and near, for the successive race meetings in the neighbourhood.

What else remained to be done for success has been duly done by the municipal authorities both of Brighton and Hove, who show care in providing amusements and amenities, also effectual drainage, and a supply of good water, which, indeed, is rather hard, as to be expected in this chalk country.

Since we have given a plan of Brighton, it will not be necessary to do more than indicate its main features. The first goal of the stranger is likely to be the sea-side, for which, from the station, he follows a straight line, in its lower part named *West Street*, much occupied by restaurants of a popular kind, whose staff stand at the door touting for the custom of excursionists, sometimes so vigorously as if they would compel them to come in and be fed. At the top of this street a Clock Tower marks the intersection of one of the chief business thoroughfares, *North Street* and *Western Road*, running roughly parallel to the sea front, on which we debouch at the gayest part between the two piers, close to the largest hotels and most showy shops.

Opposite the bottom of *West Street*, on the shore, is a spacious hall for refuge on a wet day. Another large shelter is provided under the *Marine Parade*, a good way eastward ; and the arches beneath the upper promenades contain many refreshment rooms, places of refuge, and public conveniences. It is this care for the comfort of the temporarily homeless that makes Brighton so popular with excursionists—a feature which other resorts would do well to imitate, for what can be more miserable than a crew of drenched pleasure-seekers turned out on a wet day, with no place of free shelter? All the same, Brighton would have us know that it has fewer wet days than most places ; and the summer visitor's complaint is more like to be a dazzling sun, that may blind him to the glories of this grandest parade in the world, stretching away for about 2 miles in either direction.

The crowded part of the line of promenades, upper and lower, is about a mile long, shading off at each end into terraces of quieter dignity. It is here chiefly known as *King's Road*, the front taking different names on its various stretches. What is called the *Grand Parade* runs inland by the *Steyne Gardens*, to which we shall come presently. Westward we reach **Hove**, alias *West Brighton*, alias *Cliftonville*, which preserves its municipal independence, and gives itself airs of west end fashion. The esplanade here is broader and lower, enclosing wide *Lawns*, which are a scene of much gentility when the band plays, or on Sundays in the "church parade" hour. Eastward is reached *Kemp Town*, looked down on by roystering spirits as not so gay, but this quarter, much given to girls' schools, is by no means to be despised; and nothing could be more stately than the opening of *Lewes Crescent* and *Sussex Square*. Kemp Town boasts to be on chalk, whereas haughty Hove's foundation is not such a dry one. At the East end, the upper parade runs high, so that it might almost rank as a cliff; and towards the end there is a lift for the accommodation of weak knees. Below, on the shore, starts at the Aquarium an *Electric Railway*, now being pushed on, from Kemp Town, along the coast towards *Rottingdean*. From *Castle Square*, behind the Aquarium, omnibuses may be taken for outlying quarters; and here and hereabouts in fine weather conveyances are quickly filled for cheap drives to *Rottingdean*, the *Devil's Dyke*, and other points.

Beyond the *Aquarium*, which might be taken as a central point, projects the old *Chain Pier*, whose nose has rather been put out of joint by the more elaborate attractions of the *West Pier*. Between them another pier has been begun, meant by its "Marine Palace" to throw both into the shade; but for the present this enterprise seems to be suffering the fate of the Tower of Babel. The *West Pier* is a great resort, where are crowds, bands, entertainments, restaurants, stalls, illuminations, and all the fine fun of this Vanity Fair, besides the humbler delights of a *camera obscura*, penny-in-the-slot apparatus, and the inevitable advertisements. The Concert Room at the head will hold nearly 2000 persons. Here start two steamboats, plying on short trips in the channel or to neighbouring watering-places.

Between the piers, the wide beach is thickly covered with boats and bathing machines, and the back of it turned into a smooth roadway for donkeys and bicycles. Hourly sails for a shilling are very popular, the best known yachts being the two *Skylarks*, which, on this coast, is almost a generic name for craft of the kind. Rowing makes rather a dear diversion here, the smallest charge for a rowing boat being 2s. 6d. an hour, since the Corporation, in its paternal care for excursionists, does not allow them to venture forth but under charge of a boatman.

Restrictions as to bathing are by no means so severe as might be expected on such a frequented shore. Between the squadrons of bathing machines there are three or four parts of the beach appointed where men may bathe, morning and evening, in the very slightest costume, as may be done at any hour beside one of the groins beyond the west end of Hove. The beach is shingly on the upper part, but at low water becomes a wide stretch of sand, on which one has to walk out a long way to get into danger. Bathing from boats within a certain distance of the shore is prohibited. Swimmers may plunge from the end of the West Pier up to 1 P.M., but they must pay 6d., which seems a high charge, with an addition for the use of towels and costumes. There are several luxurious swimming and other baths—*Brill's* and *Hobden's* in King's Road, and the new *Hove Baths* in *Medina Road*, besides the Brighton *Corporation Baths* in North Street, and the *Turkish Baths* in West Street, with a gymnasium overhead.

One sight of the beach, in the morning, is the *al fresco* fish-market held about half-way between the two piers, where the fish are put up to sale by "Dutch auction," the price gradually brought down ; and retail vendors hoarsely tempt the stranger to buy his own breakfast.

In the *King's Road* above, near the bottom of *West Street*, will be found *Mutton's*, the pastry-cook's, famed as one of the oldest of Brighton restaurants, which in this part abound, with charges on various scales.

The sea and the sun being Brighton's strong points, we have spoken of its aquatic delights before going on to explore the town, with its public places and few fragments of antiquity. Returning to the Aquarium, we find the chief opening inward, the *Steyne*, a local name for "hollow" (pronounced *Steene*), where a line of fine gardens, containing the buildings of the *Pavilion*, leads up to the principal church, *St. Peter's*, behind which is a rather dusty bit of park known as the *Level*. This broad thoroughfare divides at the Church, bending off to the left as the *London Road*, to the right as the *Lewes Road*, about both of which rise the physically but not socially high quarters, shutting in the town at the back.

St. Peter's, now the Parish Church, is an early work of the late Sir Charles Barry, a stately and spacious Gothic pile, deserving its rank. The vicar has the presentation of the several district churches into which the parish is divided, Hove and adjoining parishes supplying several others, of which only a few need be particularised. *St. Bartholomew's*, a tall bare-looking building very prominent to the west of the station, and near St. Peter's, has the reputation of being the most ornate in its services. *St. Martin's*, close at hand in the Lewes Road, is remarkable for its internal decoration, especially the rood screen erected as a military monument. These and, we believe, other new churches are owed to the liberality of the venerable incumbent (Rev. A. D. Wagner) of *St. Paul's* in West Street, an old stronghold of high church practices. *Christ Church* is noted for the opposite extreme. *St. Patrick's*, Hove, is said to have the most fashionable congregation, attracted by its lively services. Worshippers of another stamp will be more interested in *Holy Trinity* (opposite the Post Office), as once scene of the ministrations of Brighton's greatest preacher, F. W. Robertson, commemorated here by a chancel window.

The old parish church of *St. Nicholas* is that most likely to be visited for mere curiosity. It stands on a hill to the south-west of the station, on the other side of which mounts *Dyke Road*, one of the chief drives out of the town. This church has been restored in memory of the great Duke of Wellington, who was once a pupil of the vicar; and there is an elaborate monument to him in the chancel.

BRIGHTON

The richly coloured east window, the gilt and painted oak screen, and the curious font, whose not unquestioned antiquity seems to have been at least retouched, are noticeable features. Out-topped by other buildings, St. Nicholas has lost its character as a sea-mark ; but there is still an open view from the churchyard. Here, not far from the eastern entrance of the church, is the prominent tomb and quaint doggerel epitaph of *Captain Nicholas Tettersell*, who carried out Charles II.'s escape. Near it is a fragment of an old stone cross, which Roundhead troopers get the blame of demolishing; also another noted tombstone to *Phœbe Hessell*, who died at the reputed age of 108, born in the reign of Queen Anne and pensioned by George IV. after serving many years as a common soldier, in which capacity the disguised heroine was wounded at Fontenoy.

On the other side of the road, an extension of the burial-ground has been laid out as a public resort, much frequented by nurses and babies, hardly able to profit by the edifying warnings that are so common on Sussex tombstones. This burial-ground, in turn, has been long outgrown ; and Brighton has now more than one cemetery on the heights above.

The *Town Hall*, with the markets opposite, stands in a square near the bottom of the Steyne. It is a heavy building, not much admired ; but a local Guide assures us that the police cells below are "light, spacious, and comfortable," if that detail be of any interest to our readers. The *Hove Town Hall* in *Church Road*, the continuation of Western Road, makes a much more successful building of red brick and terra-cotta, and contains a fine peal of bells with a carillon.

The *Royal Pavilion* presents itself as a link between the institutions of Church and State and those of mere amusement. This notorious building was a "folly" of George IV., who began it when under a Chinese craze, and rebuilt it during his regency, at a total cost of over a million, unless the temptation of rhyme betrayed Byron into exaggeration—

BRIGHTON

"Shut up—no, not the King, but the Pavilion,
Or else 'twill cost us all another million!"

The result is a curious gimcrack medley of the Chinese and the Moslem, which suggested to Sydney Smith that "the dome of St. Paul's had come to Brighton and pupped." Flattering critics have compared this monstrosity to the Taj Mehal at Agra; but Sir Walter Scott, usually indulgent enough to the failings of royalty, abused it as heartily as the sour Cobbett. The Taj has been called the most beautiful building in the world. The criticism commonly passed on the Pavilion is a very different one. Of the life led here by "the first gentleman in Europe," among his favourites and parasites, the less said the better. Mrs. Fitzherbert, his unacknowledged wife, who but for the royal marriage law might have made him a different man, had a house on the sea-side of the gardens, now occupied by the Young Men's Christian Association, where she outlived the king and died respected by his successor.

Whatever may be said of the Pavilion, the *Steyne Gardens*, extending north and south of it, are admirable, all the more so for Brighton's poverty in green and shade. In the south enclosure plays the grand *Victoria Fountain*, and the seats here are all free, so that there is no scanty audience when the band performs.

In his later days, George IV. deserted Brighton for the seclusion of Windsor Park. William IV. favoured it; but Queen Victoria found it wanting in quiet and comfort, or, as the story goes, was driven away by the intrusiveness of her neighbours. In 1849 the Pavilion was sold to the town for £53,000, and, with its gardens, makes now what would be the Casino or Kursaal of a foreign spa.

The chief apartments in the main building, open on a payment of 6d., are worth seeing for the curiosity and richness of their decorations, especially in the roof and chandeliers of the *Banqueting Hall*. The royal stables are now converted into the *Dome Assembly Hall*, holding

3000 people. The former Riding School is the *Corn Exchange*. Fêtes, concerts, balls, flower-shows, and other gatherings, from banquets to prayer-meetings, are held in the rooms and the grounds.

Another part of the building, opening into *Church Street*, is used for a *Free Library, Museum*, and *Picture Gallery*, the last containing some good pictures, and not less than three portraits of George IV., as patron saint of Brighton, whose statue duly stands in the grounds, as does one of Sir Cordy Burrows, an energetic mayor to whom the town owes much. The *Museum* (free) has a fine collection of porcelain, and another of weapons. The collections of curiosities in the show-rooms of the Pavilion should also have been mentioned. And we must not omit the *Booth Museum of British Stuffed Birds* (in the *Dyke Road*), said to be the best of the kind in England, but open free to the public.

Next to the Pavilion, among places of entertainment, must rank the *Aquarium*, sunk below the level of the esplanade in a manner that gives no idea of its resources. But for this unobtrusive situation, it might be called the Crystal Palace of Brighton. The whole length of the building is 700 feet. Besides the well-stocked tanks that are its *raison d'être*, it has a stage, organ, conservatory, news-room, restaurant, shooting gallery, billiard tables, and other attractions, to which the charge for admission is 1s., or 6d. in the evening and to excursionists on production of railway ticket. At the west end of the *Aquarium* are at present only the beginnings of the new pier and *Marine Palace*, which, if brought to completion, will add a new resort to Brighton's amenities.

The *Theatre Royal* is to the west of the Pavilion, in New Road. The performances are apt to be of the usual provincial order; but for the Thursday afternoon *matinées*, first-class companies often come down from London. What would there be called the "Transpontine" drama finds a home at the *Gaiety Theatre* in the north quarter of Brighton, towards the barracks. The *Alhambra* in King's Road, the *Empire*, beside the Theatre Royal, and the *Eden* (late *Ginnett's Circus*) in North Road, are for "variety" performances. The *Grand Concert Hall*, at the bottom of *West Street*, is used for a skating rink in winter, and is in part a restaurant; it was in this house, according to some authorities, that Dr. Johnson lodged on his visit to Brighton with the Thrales and Fanny Burney.

This does not exhaust the list of places of amusement; and in fine weather the beach is of course much taken up by open-air performances; while it seems as if from morning till night bands were always at work in the Steyne Gardens, on the Pier, on the Lawns, or somewhere.

For parks and other open spaces, besides those already mentioned, Brighton is well off.

St. Ann's Well and *Garden* on Furze Hill, about half a mile back from Brunswick Square, make a pleasant resort, though the chalybeate water be no longer so much asked for as tea and other refreshments. The Garden has among its attractions a monkey house, containing a lively representation of the death and burial of Cock Robin, which, like that at Bramber, will not fail to delight young folks. Ground for tennis and other sports are provided for school parties; and a peep at this oasis of green shade in the desert of bricks and stucco is worth the charge for admission (3d.; on Sundays 6d., or by season tickets). Omnibuses along the *Western Road* would put one down close to the entrance.

Preston Park, in the north-western suburb, forms a large and agreeable recreation ground of 72 acres, the upper part containing a roomy arena for matches and sports, with banked seats. In the lower part there are tennis courts, to be hired by the hour, as on the sea-front and elsewhere. Polo also is played here. While in this suburb, we must call attention to (near the north-west corner of the Park) the old church of *St. Peter*, restored, the walls of the nave showing in rude fresco the murder of Thomas à Becket. Between this outskirt of Brighton and the Downs are some finely shaded bits of road, a feature not too common hereabouts.

BRIGHTON

The *Queen's Park*, near the Kemp Town station and below the *Racecourse* on the Downs, is a smaller pleasure-ground for this end of the town. At the top of it will be seen a curious tower known as the "Pepper-box." At the bottom is the *German Spa*, a manufactory of artificial mineral waters, whose grand facade hints at an intended consumption on the premises, belied by its grass-grown walks.

The *Hove Recreation Park* and the *County Cricket Ground* in Selborne Road are open spaces of the west end; and at the back of the town, bits of "eligible building land" are still available for youth to *prendre ses ébats*. Brighton, though playgrounds must be rather at a premium here, is well known as a great place for education. There are said to be 300 schools for boys and girls, who, for the most part, look as if the air suited them better than it did poor Paul Dombey, or as if they did not "resume their studies" with such blighting intensity. A house on the Marine Parade is pointed out as the original of Dr. Blimber's establishment. *Brighton College*, at the same end, takes the lead among the schools of all classes.

For elders who find it not so easy to take exercise, a *Marine Drive*, 7 miles long, has been opened up round the back of the town, running from *Rottingdean* on the east side, to *Aldrington* on the west, where there is talk of erecting an *Eiffel Tower* to command the prospect. Not that the environs of Brighton are destitute of natural view points. Above it are two British hill forts—*Hollingbury* in Patcham parish, over 500 feet high, and about a mile behind Preston; then, nearer, and more to the east, *White Hawk* at the end of the Racecourse.

Before leaving the town, we must call attention to two very different features of note, in the labyrinth of old lanes still to be threaded about *North Street*, where bargains in the way of curiosities may sometimes be picked up; and in the new avenues leading from the Hove sea-front, by which an attempt has been made to remove the reproach of treelessness brought against the "queen of watering-places."

Andrew Gill: I have collected historical photographs and optical antiques for over forty years. I am a professional 'magic lantern' showman presenting Victorian slide shows and giving talks on early optical entertainments for museums, festivals, special interest groups and universities. Please visit my website '**Magic Lantern World**' at www.magiclanternist.com

My booklets and photo albums are available from Amazon, simply search for the titles below. If you've enjoyed this book, please leave a review on Amazon, as good ratings are very important to independent authors. If you're disappointed, please let me know the reason, so that I can address the issue in future editions.

Historical travel guides
New York
Jersey in 1921
Norwich in 1880
Doon the Watter
Liverpool in 1886
Nottingham in 1899
Bournemouth in 1914
Great Yarmouth in 1880
Victorian Walks in Surrey
The Way We Were: Bath
A Victorian Visit to Brighton
The Way We Were: Lincoln
A Victorian Visit to Hastings
A Victorian Visit to Falmouth
Newcastle upon Tyne in 1903
Victorian and Edwardian York
The Way We Were: Llandudno
A Victorian Visit to North Devon
The Way We Were: Manchester
A Victorian Guide to Birmingham
Leeds through the Magic Lantern
An Edwardian Guide to Leicester
Victorian and Edwardian Bradford
Victorian and Edwardian Sheffield

The Way We Were: North Cornwall
A Victorian Visit to Fowey and Looe
A Victorian Visit to Peel, Isle of Man
Doncaster through the Magic Lantern
The Way We Were: The Lake District
Lechlade to Oxford by Canoe in 1875
Guernsey, Sark and Alderney in 1921
East Devon through the Magic Lantern
The River Thames from Source to Sea
A Victorian Visit to Ramsey, Isle of Man
A Victorian Visit to Douglas, Isle of Man
Victorian Totnes through the Magic Lantern
Victorian Whitby through the Magic Lantern
Victorian London through the Magic Lantern
St. Ives through the Victorian Magic Lantern
Victorian Torquay through the Magic Lantern
Victorian Glasgow through the Magic Lantern
The Way We Were: Wakefield and Dewsbury
The Way We Were: Hebden Bridge to Halifax
Victorian Blackpool through the Magic Lantern
Victorian Scarborough through the Magic Lantern
The Way We Were: Hull and the Surrounding Area
The Way We Were: Harrogate and Knaresborough
A Victorian Tour of North Wales: Rhyl to Llandudno
A Victorian Visit to Lewes and the surrounding area
The Isle of Man through the Victorian Magic Lantern
A Victorian Visit to Helston and the Lizard Peninsula
A Victorian Railway Journey from Plymouth to Padstow
A Victorian Visit to Barmouth and the Surrounding Area
The Way We Were: Holmfirth, Honley and Huddersfield
A Victorian Visit to Malton, Pickering and Castle Howard
A Victorian Visit to Eastbourne and the surrounding area
A Victorian Visit to Aberystwyth and the Surrounding Area
The Way We Were: Rotherham and the Surrounding Area
A Victorian Visit to Castletown, Port St. Mary and Port Erin
Penzance and Newlyn through the Victorian Magic Lantern
A Victorian Journey to Snowdonia, Caernarfon and Pwllheli
Victorian Brixham and Dartmouth through the Magic Lantern
Victorian Plymouth and Devonport through the Magic Lantern
A Victorian Tour of North Wales: Conwy to Caernarfon via Anglesey
Staithes, Runswick and Robin Hood's Bay through the Magic Lantern
Dawlish, Teignmouth and Newton Abbot through the Victorian Magic Lantern

Walking Books
Victorian Edinburgh Walks
Victorian Rossendale Walks
More Victorian Rossendale Walks
Victorian Walks on the Isle of Wight (Book 1)

Victorian Walks on the Isle of Wight (Book 2)
Victorian Rossendale Walks: The End of an Era

Other historical topics
The YMCA in the First World War
Sarah Jane's Victorian Tour of Scotland
The River Tyne through the Magic Lantern
The 1907 Wrench Cinematograph Catalogue
Victorian Street Life through the Magic Lantern
The First World War through the Magic Lantern
Ballyclare May Fair through the Victorian Magic Lantern
The Story of Burnley's Trams through the Magic Lantern
The Franco-British 'White City' London Exhibition of 1908
The 1907 Wrench 'Optical and Science Lanterns' Catalogue
The CWS Crumpsall Biscuit Factory through the Magic Lantern
How They Built the Forth Railway Bridge: A Victorian Magic Lantern Show

Historical photo albums (just photos)
The Way We Were: Suffolk
Norwich: The Way We Were
The Way We Were: Somerset
Fife through the Magic Lantern
York through the Magic Lantern
Rossendale: The Way We Were
The Way We Were: Cumberland
Burnley through the Magic Lantern
Oban to the Hebrides and St. Kilda
Tasmania through the Magic Lantern
Swaledale through the Magic Lantern
Llandudno through the Magic Lantern
Birmingham through the Magic Lantern
Penzance, Newlyn and the Isles of Scilly
Great Yarmouth through the Magic Lantern
Ancient Baalbec through the Magic Lantern
The Isle of Skye through the Magic Lantern
Ancient Palmyra through the Magic Lantern
The Kentish Coast from Whitstable to Hythe
New South Wales through the Magic Lantern
From Glasgow to Rothesay by Paddle Steamer
Victorian Childhood through the Magic Lantern
The Way We Were: Yorkshire Railway Stations
Southampton, Portsmouth and the Great Liners
Newcastle upon Tyne through the Magic Lantern
Egypt's Ancient Monuments through the Magic Lantern
The Way We Were: Birkenhead, Port Sunlight and the Wirral
Ancient Egypt, Baalbec and Palmyra through the Magic Lantern

Copyright © 2021 by Andrew Gill. All rights reserved.
No part of this book may be reproduced or used in any manner without written permission of the copyright owner.

Contact email: victorianhistory@virginmedia.com

Printed in Great Britain
by Amazon